# ZEN
# WISDOM

# ZEN WISDOM

Classic Buddhist Teachings to Calm the Mind

ABBIE HEADON

Copyright © 2025 Amber Books Ltd

Amber Books Ltd
United House
North Road
London N7 9DP
United Kingdom

www.amberbooks.co.uk
Facebook: amberbooks
YouTube: amberbooksltd
Instagram: amberbooksltd
X(Twitter): @amberbooks

All rights reserved. No part of this work may be reproduced,
stored in a retrieval system, or transmitted in any form or by
any means, electronic, mechanical, photocopying, recording,
or otherwise, without the prior permission of the copyright holder.

ISBN: 978-1-83886-511-5

Project Editor: Anna Brownbridge
Designer: Mark Batley
Picture Research: Terry Forshaw

Printed and bound in China

---

TRADITIONAL CHINESE BOOKBINDING
This book has been produced using traditional Chinese bookbinding
techniques, using a method that was developed during the Ming Dynasty
(1368–1644) and remained in use until the adoption of Western binding
techniques in the early 1900s. In traditional Chinese binding, single sheets of
paper are printed on one side only, and each sheet is folded in half, with the
printed pages on the outside. The book block is then sandwiched between
two boards and sewn together through punched holes close to the cut edges
of the folded sheets.

# Contents

INTRODUCTION 6

ON TRANQUILITY 8

ON PURPOSE 19

ON CONCENTRATION 30

ON MINDFULNESS 41

ON JOY AND HAPPINESS 52

ON LEARNING 63

ON HELPING OTHERS 74

ON DEATH 85

PICTURE CREDITS 96

# Introduction

*"Zen is not some special state, it is our normal condition –
silent, peaceful, awake, without agitation."*
– TAISEN DESHIMARU

The word 'zen' has come to mean something rather broad in the English language: 'I just wish I could be more zen about this,' I say about a small but irritating problem, 'but it's really winding me up.' In this case, 'zen' with a small 'z' refers to a calmer approach to life that doesn't sweat the small stuff. Maybe we could all do with being a bit more zen in this sense of the word.

But 'Zen', with a capital Z, means so much more than this. Its roots stretch back to South Asia, with the birth of Buddhism 2500 years ago. Buddhism teaches that suffering is a part of life, caused by our innate tendency to cling to habits and beliefs and to crave what we do not have. Followers of Buddhism seek to free themselves from this suffering by following a path towards enlightenment, or awakening – in fact, the very word 'Buddha' means 'awakened one'. This anthology of quotations includes several words of wisdom from Siddhartha Gautama, the Buddha, whose words have inspired millions of people since he started teaching 'the Middle Way', a way of life that avoids extremes of self-indulgence and self-denial, in the fifth century BCE.

# INTRODUCTION

A key concept in Buddhism is *dhyāna*, a Sanskrit word describing a meditative state, and when Buddhism spread to China this word transformed into *Chán*. From the seventh century CE, Chinese teachers travelled to Japan and Japanese monks journeyed to China, and new schools of Zen Buddhism – with 'Zen' being a Japanese evolution of the word Chán – branched out and became established in Japan. The first independent Japanese Zen school was founded in the twelfth century CE, and Zen went on to spread across the country. Today, there are around 15,000 Zen temples in Japan, and over five million Japanese people follow Zen practices.

One of the most important figures in the early history of Zen in Japan is Dōgen Zenji (1200–1253). As a young man, he travelled to China, and on his return he wrote a treatise about the importance of *zazen*, or sitting meditation. He went on to establish his own community, the Sōtō school of Zen, which is still active today. You will find quotations from Dōgen Zenji in this collection, along with words of guidance and encouragement from many other Japanese Zen teachers, including Ryōkan Taigu (1758–1831), Kōdō Sawaki (1880–1965), Shunryū Suzuki (1904–1971), Kōshō Uchiyama (1912–1998) and Taisen Deshimaru (1914–1982).

Meditation is the fundamental practice at the heart of Zen Buddhism. The word 'practice' is important here, because Zen is based on the principle that the act of meditation is more important than any particular set of beliefs. Zen is not so much something you believe, as something you *do*: by calming the body and mind, meditation can become a pathway to freedom and enlightenment. As Dōgen Zenji himself said, 'The way of Zen is to be awake and aware, to be mindful of the present moment and to live in the present moment.'

ON TRANQUILITY

"You find peace not by rearranging the circumstances
of your life, but by realising who you are
at the deepest level."

– Eckhart Tolle

# ON TRANQUILITY

"As a bee gathering nectar does not harm
or disturb the colour and fragrance of the flower;
so do the wise move through the world."

– BUDDHA

ON TRANQUILITY

"The more we attune to peace,
the more radiant our lives become."

– ZEN PROVERB

# ON TRANQUILITY

"The goal of Zen is to find peace
in the midst of chaos."

– Taisen Deshimaru

ON TRANQUILITY

"Sitting quietly, doing nothing, spring comes,
and the grass grows by itself."

– ZEN PROVERB

## ON TRANQUILITY

"Peace comes from within.
Do not seek it without."

– BUDDHA

ON TRANQUILITY

"Silence is the gateway to the infinite."

– Ryōkan Taigu

## ON TRANQUILITY

"To be calm is the highest achievement of the self."

– Shunryū Suzuki

ON TRANQUILITY

"The beauty of Zen is found in simplicity and tranquillity, in a sense of the all-embracing harmony of things."

– Thích Thiên-Ân

ON TRANQUILITY

"Quiet the mind and the soul will speak."

– Buddha

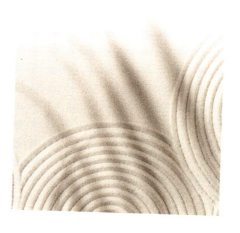

## ON TRANQUILITY

"Zen is not some special state, it is our normal condition, silent, peaceful, awake, without agitation."

– TAISEN DESHIMARU

ON PURPOSE

"Do not follow the idea of others,
but learn to listen to the voice within yourself."

– Dōgen Zenji

ON PURPOSE

"Only when you can be extremely pliable
and soft can you be extremely hard and strong."

– Zen proverb

ON PURPOSE

"The true purpose of life is
to awaken to our true nature."

– Kōdō Sawaki

ON PURPOSE

"Have the fearless attitude of a hero
and the loving heart of a child."

– Soyen Shaku

ON PURPOSE

"Move and the way will open."

– Zen Proverb

ON PURPOSE

"Finding and living in alignment with the inner purpose is the foundation for your outer purpose."

– Eckhart Tolle

ON PURPOSE

"Touch the hole in your life,
and there flowers will bloom."

– Zen proverb

ON PURPOSE

"Irrigators channel waters; fletchers straighten arrows; carpenters bend wood; the wise master themselves."

– Buddha

ON PURPOSE

"The purpose of life is not to accumulate wealth
or fame, but to find meaning and purpose
in our own existence."

– Ryōkan Taigu

ON PURPOSE

"For Zen students a weed is a treasure.
With this attitude, whatever you do,
life becomes an art."

– Shunryū Suzuki

ON PURPOSE

"Set your heart on doing good.
Do it over and over again,
And you will be filled with joy."

– Buddha

## ON CONCENTRATION

"Before enlightenment, chop wood, carry water,
after enlightenment chop wood, carry water."

– Zen proverb

# ON CONCENTRATION

"The best way to control your mind
is to not control it at all."

– Taisen Deshimaru

## ON CONCENTRATION

"Zen is not some kind of excitement,
but concentration on our usual everyday routine."

– Shunryū Suzuki

# ON CONCENTRATION

"The whole moon and the entire sky are reflected in one dewdrop on the grass."

– Dōgen Zenji

# ON CONCENTRATION

"All true artists, whether they know it or not,
create from a place of no-mind, from inner stillness."

– Eckhart Tolle

# ON CONCENTRATION

"Zen is an effort to become alert and awake."

– Osho

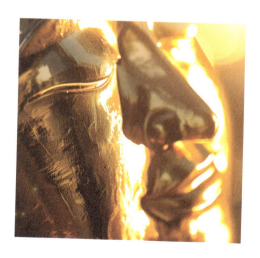

# ON CONCENTRATION

"Think with your whole body."

– Taisen Deshimaru

## ON CONCENTRATION

"If you are unable to find the truth right where you are, where else do you expect to find it?"

– Dōgen Zenji

ON CONCENTRATION

"When you do something,
you should burn yourself up completely,
like a good bonfire, leaving no trace of yourself."

– Shunryū Suzuki

# ON CONCENTRATION

"If we could see the miracle of a single flower clearly,
our whole life would change."

– BUDDHA

## ON CONCENTRATION

"We must learn to be fully present in each moment, rather than constantly distracted by our thoughts and emotions."

– Kōshō Uchiyama

## ON MINDFULNESS

"Mindfulness is not about getting anywhere else
– it's about being where you are and knowing it."

– Jon Kabat-Zinn

ON MINDFULNESS

"It is in the present
and only in the present that you live.
There is no other reality than present reality."

– ALAN WATTS

ON MINDFULNESS

"The present moment is our doorway to liberation."

– Pema Chödrön

ON MINDFULNESS

"You should sit in meditation for twenty minutes
every day – unless you're too busy;
then you should sit for an hour."

– Zen proverbi

ON MINDFULNESS

"Meditation is the best medicine for the mind."

– Kōdō Sawaki

ON MINDFULNESS

"It all depends on you.
You can go on sleeping forever,
you can wake up right this moment."

– Osho

ON MINDFULNESS

"Awareness is the power that is concealed
within the present moment."

– Eckhart Tolle

ON MINDFULNESS

"The practice of Zen is forgetting the self
in the act of uniting with something."

– KOUN YAMADA

ON MINDFULNESS

"When a garden is used as a place to pause
for thought, that is when a Zen garden comes to life.
When you contemplate a garden like this it will form
as lasting impression on your heart."

– Zen proverb

ON MINDFULNESS

"Meditation is the art of letting go of everything except what's truly important."

– Kōdō Sawaki

## ON MINDFULNESS

"The way of Zen is to be awake and aware,
to be mindful of the present moment,
and to live in the present moment."

– Dōgen Zenji

ON JOY AND HAPPINESS

"Pleasure is always derived
from something outside you,
whereas joy arises from within."

– Eckhart Tolle

# ON JOY AND HAPPINESS

"Man suffers only because he takes seriously
what the gods made for fun."

– ALAN WATTS

ON JOY AND HAPPINESS

"There is no way to happiness;
happiness is the way."

– Thích Nhat Hanh

ON JOY AND HAPPINESS

"One loses joy and happiness
in the attempt to possess them."

– Masanobu Fukuoka

ON JOY AND HAPPINESS

"Happiness is simple.
Everything we do to find it is complicated."

– Karen Maezen Miller

ON JOY AND HAPPINESS

"There is no need to search;
achievement leads to nowhere.
It makes no difference at all,
so just be happy now!
Love is the only reality of the world."

– Dōgen Zenji

ON JOY AND HAPPINESS

"The key to true happiness
is not in accumulating more things,
but in finding contentment
with what we have."

– Kōshō Uchiyama

ON JOY AND HAPPINESS

"When we are truly present in the moment,
we can appreciate the beauty of life
and find joy in simple things."

– Kōshō Uchiyama

ON JOY AND HAPPINESS

"If with a pure mind a person speaks or acts,
happiness follows them
like a never-departing shadow."

– Buddha

ON JOY AND HAPPINESS

"The journey itself is my home.
Do not seek to follow in the footsteps of the wise;
seek what they sought."

– Matsuo Bashō

ON JOY AND HAPPINESS

"The only way to be truly happy
is to let go of everything."

– Kōdō Sawaki

ON LEARNING

"Children are natural Zen masters;
their world is brand new
in each and every moment."

– JOHN BRADSHAW

ON LEARNING

"The mind of the beginner is empty,
free of the habits of the expert,
ready to accept, to doubt,
and open to all the possibilities."

— SHUNRYŪ SUZUKI

ON LEARNING

"Knowledge is learning something new every day.
Wisdom is letting go of something every day."

– Zen proverb

ON LEARNING

"Nothing ever goes away
until it has taught us what we need to know."

– Pema Chödrön

ON LEARNING

"To study the self is to forget the self.
To forget the self is to be enlightened
by the ten thousand things."

– Dōgen Zenji

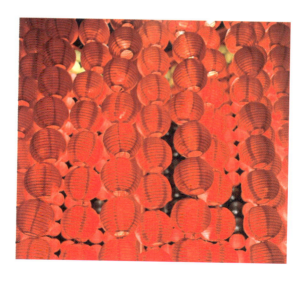

ON LEARNING

"The true teacher is not the one
who has all the answers,
but the one who guides us
to find them within ourselves."

– Ryōkan Taigu

ON LEARNING

"'To travel is to be alive,
but to get somewhere is to be dead,'
for as our own proverb says,
'To travel well is better than to arrive.'"

– ALAN WATTS

ON LEARNING

"Do not think you will necessarily be aware
of your own enlightenment."

– Dōgen Zenji

ON LEARNING

To follow the path, look to the master,
follow the master, walk with the master,
see through the master, become the master."

– Zen proverb

ON LEARNING

"For things to reveal themselves to us,
we need to be ready to abandon our views about them."

– Thích Nhat Hanh

## ON LEARNING

"We are all here to learn, to grow,
and to help others on their own journey."

– Ryōkan Taigu

ON HELPING OTHERS

"For the good of the many,
for the happiness of the many,
out of compassion for the world."

– BUDDHA

ON HELPING OTHERS

"To receive everything,
one must open one's hands and give."

– TAISEN DESHIMARU

ON HELPING OTHERS

"Our prime purpose in this life is to help others.
And if you can't help them, at least don't hurt them."

– Dalai Lama

ON HELPING OTHERS

"If in our daily life we can smile,
if we can be peaceful and happy,
not only we,
but everyone will profit from it."

– Thích Nhat Hanh

ON HELPING OTHERS

"Nothing ever exists entirely alone.
Everything is in relation to everything else."

– BUDDHA

ON HELPING OTHERS

"If you want to change the world,
start with the next person who comes to you in need."

– B. D. Schiers

ON HELPING OTHERS

"By listening with calm and understanding, we can ease the suffering of another person."

– Thích Nhat Hanh

## ON HELPING OTHERS

"We work on ourselves in order to help others,
but also we help others
in order to work on ourselves."

– PEMA CHÖDRÖN

ON HELPING OTHERS

"Throwing away Zen mind is correct Zen mind.
Only keep the question 'What is the best way
of helping other people?'"

– SEUNGSAHN HAENGWON

ON HELPING OTHERS

"Teach this triple truth to all:
A generous heart, kind speech,
and a life of service and compassion
are the things which renew humanity."

– BUDDHA

ON HELPING OTHERS

"Be kind whenever possible. It is always possible."

– DALAI LAMA

ON DEATH

"To live in the realm of Buddha nature
means to die as a small self
and to be reborn as a universal self."

– SHUNRYŪ SUZUKI

ON DEATH

"We must learn to accept the impermanence
of all things, and find peace in the midst of change."

– Kōshō Uchiyama

ON DEATH

"Whatever has the nature of arising
has the nature of ceasing."

– BUDDHA

ON DEATH

"Forget the years, forget distinctions.
Leap into the boundless
and make it your home."

– ZHUANGZI

ON DEATH

"Everything that has a beginning has an ending.
Make your peace with that and all will be well."

– JACK KOENFIELD

ON DEATH

"Until you stop breathing,
there's more right with you
than wrong with you."

– Jon Kabat-Zinn

ON DEATH

"Treat every moment as your last.
It is not preparation for something else."

– Shunryū Suzuki

# ON DEATH

"The way out of life and death
is not some special technique;
essential thing is to penetrate
to the root of life and death."

– Bukko

ON DEATH

"The ultimate goal of Zen is not to escape suffering, but to transform it into wisdom and compassion."

– Kōshō Uchiyama

ON DEATH

"One must be deeply aware
of the impermanence of the world."

– Dōgen Zenji

ON DEATH

"In the end, only three things matter:
how much you loved,
how gently you lived,
and how gracefully you let go of things
not meant for you."

– BUDDHA

# Picture Credits

**Alamy:** 9 (Pictures Now), 28 (Troy Doney), 44 (Eric Lafforgue), 53 (mauritius images), 68 (Keith Levit)

**Dreamstime:** 6 (Agit77), 12 (Fotogotrek), 13 (Jovani Carlo Gorospe), 16 (Christophe Villedieu), 20 (Juliengrondin), 25 (Anatoly Tiplyashin), 26 (Nitsuki), 27 (Hupeng), 29 (Telnyawka), 30 (Sascha Winter), 31 (Roman Sahaidachnyi), 33 (Chalermpon Poungpeth), 34 (Irina Kryvasheina), 35 (Altitudevs), 37 (Si Li), 40 (Cary Peterson), 45 (Anna Om), 47 (Worldtraveler46), 49 (Prostockstudio), 52 (Per Bjorkdahl), 56 (Subbotina), 57 (Wong Yu Liang), 58 (Patryk Kosmider), 61 (Satori13), 62 (Solarseven), 65 (Korn Vitthayanukarun), 67 (Videowokart), 71 (Dmitrii Melnikov), 73 (Pavel Losevsky), 75 (Alina Demchyshyna), 76 (Blazej lyjak), 81 (Xubang Yang), 85 (Juha Sompinmaki), 86 (Dampoint), 87 (Aberrant Realities)

**Getty Images:** 14 (Roberto Moiola/Sysaworld), 24 (Martin Puddy), 41 (Grant Faint), 48 (Abstract Aerial Art), 64 (d3sign)

**iStock:** 10 (kool99), 19 (Andrew_Mayovskyy), 21 (ipopba), 22 (Oleh Slobodeniuk), 32 (Yuliya Taba), 36 (Kerkez), 39 (LordRunar), 42 (WLDavies), 50, 51 (Sand555), 54 (AscentXmedia), 55 (gan chaonan), 66 (Alberto Sánchez Cerrato), 70 (Pramote2015), 74 (worradirek), 77 (hadynyah), 78 (zhongguo), 79 (PeopleImages), 80 (Oleh Slobodeniuk), 82 (Mongkolchon Akesin), 83 (ugurhan), 84 (mediaphotos), 90 (PhotoBeaM), 91 (Paolo Gagliardi), 92 (S Hoss), 93 (golero), 94 (Henrik A Jonsson), 95 (sharply done)

**Shutterstock:** 5 (Black Fabric), 8 (Belight), 11 (peterschreiber.media), 15 (Oksana Shchelkanova), 17 (Yrabota), 18 (Sofiaworld), 23 (Sergii Rudiuk), 38 (Vibe Images), 43 (Stockbym), 46 (Sai Chan), 59 (biothailand), 60 (Natalya Pyrogova), 63 (hxdbzxy), 69 (Black Fabric), 72 (KieferPix), 88 (chuyuss), 89 (helloRuby)